DESIGNING
Inclusive
Communities

Design Thinking

for a Better World

Rachel Stuckey

CRABTREE
PUBLISHING COMPANY
WWW.CRABTREEBOOKS.COM

Author: Rachel Stuckey

Series research and development:
 Reagan Miller and Janine Deschenes

Editor: Leanne Rancourt

Editorial director: Kathy Middleton

Editorial services: Clarity Content Services

Proofreader: Angela Kaelberer

Production coordinator and prepress technician:
 Tammy McGarr

Print coordinator: Katherine Berti

Cover design: Tammy McGarr

Design: David Montle

Photo Research: Linda Tanaka

Photo Credits:
Cover: TerryJ (bottom right) / iStock; Imfoto (top right) / Shutterstock; Peter Braakmann (centre left) / Shutterstock; p4 Rawpixel/shutterstock; p5 Photos courtesy of Luke Anderson of Stop Gap; p6 Jacob Lund/fotolia; p7 Rawpixel/shutterstock; p8 Photographee.eu/shutterstock; p9 Monkey Business Images/shutterstock; p10 REDPIXEL.PL/shutterstock; p11 left Monkey Business Images/shutterstock, Nejron Photo/shutterstock; p12 top Billion Photos/shutterstock, Africa Studio/shutterstock; p13 Rawpixel/shutterstock; p14 Sergey Novikov/shutterstock; p15 top Pumikan Sawatroj/Dreamstime, ronstik/shuttterstock; pp16-17 wave break media/MaXximages; p18 Vitchanan Photography/shutterstock; p19 Tim Gray/shutterstock; p20 top Look Studio/shutterstock, Monkey Business Images/shutterstock; p21 EnableTalk; p22 william casey/shutterstock; p23 AP Photo/Nam Y. Huh/The Canadian Press; p25, 26 Rawpixel/shutterstock; p27 Jacob Lund/fotolia; p28 top LightField Studios/shutterstock, De Visu/shutterstock; p29 Nyul/Dreamstime; p30 Paul Vasarhely/shutterstock; p31 Ander Dylan/shutterstock; p32 Adam Wasilewsk/shutterstock; p33 Aspen Photo/shutterstock; p34 Marmaduke St. John/Alamy/All Canada Photos; p35 Jacob Lund/fotolia; p36 meunierd/shutterstock; p37 aspen rock/shutterstock; p38 Photographee.eu/shutterstock; p39 Monkey Business Images/shutterstock; p40 Anna Krivitskaia/Dreamstime; p41 Justaman/shutterstock; p42 wavebreakmedia/shutterstock; p43 Jacob Lund/fotolia; p44 pryzmat/shutterstock.

Library and Archives Canada Cataloguing in Publication

Stuckey, Rachel, author
     Designing inclusive communities / Rachel Stuckey.

(Design thinking for a better world)
Includes bibliographical references and index.
Issued in print and electronic formats.
ISBN 978-0-7787-4460-3 (hardcover).--
ISBN 978-0-7787-4464-1 (softcover).--
ISBN 978-1-4271-2035-9 (HTML)

     1. Community development--Juvenile literature. 2. Social integration--Juvenile literature. 3. Community life--Juvenile literature. 4. Social participation--Juvenile literature. 5. Political participation--Juvenile literature. I. Title.

HN49.C6S79 2018   j307.1'4   C2017-908088-1
                                                          C2017-908089-X

Library of Congress Cataloging-in-Publication Data

Names: Stuckey, Rachel, author.
Title: Designing inclusive communities / Rachel Stuckey.
Description: New York : Crabtree Publishing Company, [2018] |
   Series: Design thinking for a better world |
   Includes bibliographical references and index.
Identifiers: LCCN 2017060080 (print) | LCCN 2018010917 (ebook) |
   ISBN 9781427120359 (Electronic) |
   ISBN 9780778744603 (hardcover) |
   ISBN 9780778744641 (pbk.)
Subjects: LCSH: Equality--Juvenile literature. | Social planning--
   Juvenile literature.
Classification: LCC HM821 (ebook) | LCC HM821 .S775 2018 (print) |
   DDC 305--dc23
LC record available at https://lccn.loc.gov/2017060080

Crabtree Publishing Company

www.crabtreebooks.com   1-800-387-7650

Printed in the U.S.A./052018/CG20180309

Published in Canada
Crabtree Publishing
616 Welland Ave.
St. Catharines, Ontario
L2M 5V6

Published in the United States
Crabtree Publishing
PMB 59051
350 Fifth Avenue, 59th Floor
New York, New York 10118

Published in the United Kingdom
Crabtree Publishing
Maritime House
Basin Road North, Hove
BN41 1WR

Published in Australia
Crabtree Publishing
3 Charles Street
Coburg North
VIC, 3058

Contents

What Is Design Thinking?

esign thinking is a problem-solving process that inspires **collaboration** and **community** involvement. Design thinking begins with empathy. Empathy is the ability to understand the feelings and perspectives of other people.

In design thinking, starting with empathy means that design thinkers try to understand the unique perspective of their user, or the person who is experiencing a problem, before designing a solution that will help them. The process aims to solve problems the user experiences in a way that works best for the user, not the designer. Design thinking can be used to create objects such as tools or devices. It can also be used to create systems and processes, or ways of doing things.

Design thinking brings many minds together to create important solutions to problems in communities, such as improving the lives of people in need by helping a local shelter.

Failing Forward

Design thinkers test their solutions with the users to see how well it works for them. Sometimes, a design thinker's solution does not work the first time. Design thinkers then change and test their solution until it works well for their user. This is called **failing forward**. Failing forward is important in design thinking, because the design-thinking process is iterative. This means it is done over and over until designers find an idea that works. Each iteration, or loop, through the process helps design thinkers improve their ideas.

Why Design Thinking?

Design thinking is often used by businesses to help create products and services that meet customers' needs. But design thinking can also be used to help people in your community. Sometimes design thinking is known as public-interest design—it is useful for solving problems for the good of others. Design thinking works best in groups and teams.

Luke Anderson Stopped the Gap

When Luke Anderson was **paralyzed** in an accident and lost the use of his legs, he learned how hard everyday life is for people who use wheelchairs. He was frustrated because he was often unable to go into certain places, usually because buildings had steps and no wheelchair-accessible ramps. This frustration helped him develop empathy for other people with mobility challenges. He realized how people with different physical abilities were affected by the lack of access to certain buildings and places. He used this empathy to design the Stop Gap, a simple, portable ramp that can be easily placed at the entrance of any building that is not wheelchair-accessible.

Luke now runs an elementary school program that is available to any school that wants to use it. Students learn about the importance of accessibility and inclusion, and about using empathy to help make their communities even better places to live. The students look for non-accessible stores and restaurants in their community and write letters to the businesses offering to help them get a Stop Gap ramp.

Installing a Stop Gap ramp is a simple way to make buildings **accessible** to wheelchair users.

The design-thinking process is a set of steps that design thinkers can follow to support creative problem solving. The process helps design thinkers to tackle big problems and develop user-centered solutions. There are a few different versions of the process, but all of them start with empathy by putting the users' needs first. The design-thinking process we will use in this book has six steps:

1. Empathize
Develop a deep understanding of the user's needs.

2. Define
Identify the user's point of view and define a problem to solve.

3. Ideate
Generate many creative ideas as possible solutions.

4. Prototype
Build a representation or model of the best idea.

5. Test
Share prototype with user and get feedback.

6. Reflect
Evaluate how well the solution met the user's needs.

Community Connections

A community is a group of people who live, work, and play together. Inclusive communities give all of its members a place and a voice. Achieving this goal requires people to problem solve to remove barriers that can exclude members of a community.

This book guides you through the design-thinking process step by step. Case studies

In an inclusive community, all members can participate. Participation is the act of being involved in something. Community participation can take many forms, including giving one's time and talent to benefit others or taking part in sports, youth groups, local celebrations, and other events.

expand your understanding of some of the barriers that can exclude and disconnect community members. You will apply the process to develop user-centered ways to connect all of the people in a community.

Mindset Tips

Be Positive	Have a positive attitude and be confident in your ability to create solutions that will improve situations.
Say Yes	There are no bad ideas. An idea may seem wild or "out there" at first, but it may lead you in new directions.
Be Brave	Don't let fear of failing stop you from being **innovative**.
Take a Break	It is helpful to look at a problem with fresh eyes.
Mix It Up!	Team up with people you don't usually work with. Different perspectives can energize a group.

Empathize

Understanding Empathy

Empathy helps design thinkers understand the problem through the user's eyes. It is the first step in design thinking and the most important part of the process.

Design thinkers use empathy when listening to the perspective of a person who is affected by a problem. This is sometimes called need finding. A need is anything that a person or group of people might require. Empathy is important because understanding a person's feelings, beliefs, and values helps us identify their needs and design solutions that will meet them.

Ask your users follow-up questions after listening closely to their responses.

Learning How to Empathize

The best way to empathize with your users is to *immerse* yourself in their lives, *engage* with them, and *observe* their lives in action. If you can, you should spend time with your users to see how they live, work, and play. Observing a community in real life is best, but you can also read about it or watch a video to observe. You can also engage users in conversation—ask questions and listen closely to their responses. Take notes about what you see and hear. But don't just use written words—take pictures, make drawings and maps, and record your users' stories on audio or video.

Shanneil's Locker

When Shanneil Turner tried out for her high school basketball team in Vacaville, California, her borrowed shoes were falling apart. She thought she wouldn't be able to play, but then she got help from her Boys and Girls Club to buy her own basketball shoes. She had been a member of the club for 10 years, so she had a place to turn to when she wanted to keep playing.

Shanneil also knew that other kids like her didn't have access to help. Her experience helped her understand that some kids don't even consider playing sports because, without assistance, buying equipment isn't possible for them. Shanneil gained empathy for others in her community who wanted to play sports but didn't have the help they needed to participate.

To help solve this problem, she started Shanneil's Locker—a program that provides new athletic shoes to middle-school and high-school students who cannot afford to buy them. To begin the Locker program, she applied for a **grant** to pay for 100 pairs of shoes and then set up a system that would get the shoes in the hands of athletes who need them.

Playing sports can be expensive, which sometimes means not all people can participate. Shanneil's Locker helps kids get the equipment they need.

Engaging to Build Empathy

You can ask your users questions to help you gain empathy. Begin by writing down some open-ended questions. Then, write down your users' answers. Pay attention to how they respond and write using their own words.

- What problems have been caused by the challenge you are facing?
- In what ways do you try to overcome these problems now?

- Describe how experiencing this challenge makes you feel.

But remember that empathy is mainly about listening. Listen closely and ask follow-up questions based on their first answers:

- Can you tell me more?
- What do you do when that happens?
- How would you change things, if you could?

Define

Defining the Need

The next step in the design-thinking process is defining a specific user and need, as well as the problem you aim to solve. The define stage helps you make sense of what you learned during the empathy stage.

In the define stage, you must **synthesize** all the information you collected. Bringing together all the information will help you identify a user who is experiencing a problem, as well as their specific need. By synthesizing information and looking for patterns and big ideas, you can see the bigger picture of a user's life and how they face challenges.

You can synthesize what you've learned by answering these questions:

- What was the most interesting thing you learned?
- What stood out the most and why?
- What patterns do you see in what you learned?
- What common ideas do you see in what you learned?

There are many ways to organize your information and identify patterns. For example, an empathy map records users' words, actions, thoughts, and feelings in separate sections. A journey map records a sequence of events or observations to help identify patterns.

TIPS:
Sticky Note Synthesis

Write each thing you learned during your empathy step on a separate sticky note, and then put the notes on a whiteboard or large wall. Move the notes around to help see the patterns. You could group related notes together, rank the notes by their importance, or arrange the notes to show cause-and-effect relationships.

Creating a Point of View

In this step of the design-thinking process we create a point-of-view (POV) statement that describes users and their needs. First, we identify the user. Then we identify their need. Based on that, and the empathy we have gained, we write a question that points us to the problem we need to solve. Together these make up our POV statement.

Who is the user?

Design thinkers must be very specific about their users. Shanneil Turner's users were students in middle school and high school from low-income families who wanted to play organized sports.

All kids should be able to participate in organized sports. How can we make that happen?

What is the user's need?

The user's need should also be clearly stated. The students Shanneil hoped to help have many needs, but in this case, the specific need Shanneil identified was athletic shoes. These students had access to sports, but they did not have access to the basic equipment—shoes—that they needed to participate.

What is the POV question?

After you've identified the users and their need, pose a POV question to help you identify the problem you will solve. Shanneil may have asked this POV question: "How might I help other students get the athletic shoes they need to participate in sports?"

Getting Started on the POV

Use this sample POV statement and question as a model when you create your own. A woman who uses a wheelchair enjoys the independence she feels when she travels around her community shopping, but she finds it hard to shop by herself at the local grocery store because she cannot reach items on the higher shelves.

POINT OF VIEW QUESTION:
How might we find a way for the woman to access the items on the higher shelves in the local grocery store?

Use these sentence prompts to help draft your POV question:

- How can we improve . . . ?
- How might we prevent . . . ?
- How can we help . . . ?

11

Generating Ideas

Now that you have defined your user's needs and your POV question, it's time to try to answer that question. In the ideate stage of the design-thinking process, we **brainstorm** solutions to the problem. This is the most exciting stage. Here, you use your imagination to come up with many different possible solutions.

The ideate stage is most effective when you work in a team. It has two parts. First you generate ideas, then you evaluate, or judge, the ideas and choose the best one to try.

Solution ideas can be physical objects, such as the Stop Gap ramp. Ideas can be a program, such as Shanneil's Locker. They can also be a process, or a different way of doing something. One online English school paired students in Brazil with senior citizens in the United States for video chats. This idea helped to address two different user needs. The Brazilian students got to practice their English.

The seniors felt good about helping other students and enjoyed the social interaction.

A solution might be a process that connects community members online.

Think Big

During the ideate stage there are no bad ideas. You should aim for generating lots of ideas and many different types of ideas—objects, programs, and processes. You should also feel free to share even ideas that seem silly. You cannot always predict what will happen during the ideate stage. Different ideas can take you and your group in different directions. Ideation can help you move beyond obvious solutions to find something that hasn't been tried already.

Time to Brainstorm

Brainstorming is the most common method of ideation. Make sure you record your ideas. Use a whiteboard or chart paper or an audio- or video-recording device. Try using both visual designs or images and words when brainstorming. Visual brainstorms can include photography or sketching. Words can include simple word webs or fishbone diagrams. It is hard to know when brainstorming is over, but setting a time limit can help make the process more effective.

When you work with others, **respect** everyone's ideas.

Narrow It Down

Once your time is up and you've brainstormed a range of ideas, you must narrow them down and then select the idea or ideas for the next step. Teams can use voting to eliminate ideas, with each member evaluating each idea based on how well they feel it would meet the user's need. Another way to choose between ideas is to organize them into different categories. Categories could be about the types of idea, such as physical, digital, or **experiential**. Categories could also be more descriptive, such as "practical or simple ideas" and "ideas that seem more complicated or difficult to create." Teams can select one idea from each category and evaluate the ideas from there. Teams should always keep the users and their need in mind when evaluating the ideas.

Prototype

Create to Demonstrate

In this stage of the design-thinking process, you will fully explore the ideas you select in the ideate stage. To explore how well an idea solves a problem, your team should build or create a prototype. This is the first model of your product or process.

Keeping It Simple

A design-thinking prototype is something that the user can test. It should be simple and easy to create. It is not meant to be a product that works like something you would buy in a store. Instead, a prototype uses inexpensive materials to demonstrate how the idea will work. Keeping it simple lets design thinkers try out several ideas without committing too much time or resources. Just like with ideation, setting a time limit can help keep the prototype stage simple and realistic. The goal is always to create something that will solve a specific user's problem.

Building a prototype is an opportunity to bring your idea to life.

Building a Prototype

Design thinkers need to show, not tell—this means they should demonstrate what they have designed, instead of telling people about what they designed. They build or create a product or process that the users can interact with, giving them a chance to provide feedback. Here are some examples of design-thinking prototypes:

- a gadget-like a tool that can grasp items on high shelves
- a model of an accessible playground
- a storyboard of a website for sharing community information
- a role-playing activity for a game that includes all classmates

To create their prototype, design thinkers might use paper and markers to explain their idea in images and words. They might use materials such as wooden craft sticks, recycled cardboard, glue, and tape to create a physical product.

Your idea might be for a new way of doing things—a process or a program. Prototypes for a process or program involve describing the idea in the clearest way possible. Descriptions or explanations should be as visual as possible and use charts, diagrams, or other media such as photography, audio, and video. A prototype could even be a script for role-playing—anything that will help users experience the idea directly.

Mapping Your Vision

Often, the solution to a need won't be a physical tool like a wheelchair ramp. Many problems today are solved using digital tools such as websites and **apps**. When design thinkers want to create a website or app, they should still show their vision as a prototype. A fast and easy way to create a prototype of a website or app idea is to use flowcharts and storyboards

on a whiteboard or chart paper. Flow charts show a step-by-step map of what website or app users will see when they click different parts of the site or app. Storyboards use pictures to show what will appear on the screen. Instead of telling users about your idea, you can use these tools to show the user what pages or screens will be included on your website or app, and what they will do and say.

Test

Putting it to the Test

In this step, design thinkers ask users to test their prototypes. Having the user test a prototype allows the designer to see how it works in practice. This helps designers improve on the idea in the next iteration, or loop, of the design-thinking process.

Sometimes it is not possible to have the user directly test a prototype. If this is the case, you can ask your peers, teachers, or family to test the prototype. Make sure that you explain to testers in detail what you learned in the empathy stage about the user's point of view, and share your POV statement and question prior to presenting your prototype to them.

The User's Experience

The best way to test an idea is to create an experience for the users. This experience could include trying out a physical object or watching a presentation of an idea or process. Whenever possible, don't tell the users what the prototype is or how to use it. Instead, let them experience and examine it. You can learn a lot by watching someone try to use or understand something for the first time.

If you present your idea to your users, use a variety of tools, such as stories and visuals, to help them understand the process.

Failing Forward

Testing is not about finding out if the user *likes* the idea, it is about finding out how the idea works or doesn't work. Think critically about your prototype and listen to the feedback from the user. This will help you identify what needs to be improved or adjusted so you can "fail forward" and make improvements in the next iteration of the process.

Testing Strategies

- Watch how users interact with the prototype and take notes.
- Ask users to "walk you through" your storyboard.
- Create a model of an everyday location that allows users to test the prototype in a safe place.
- Ask the user questions about the prototype: Was it easy to use? Was it helpful? What would would you change?
- Use a survey to collect feedback from a large group of users.

Recording Results

During the test stage, it is important that you record the feedback you receive from users. You will need to look back on this feedback in the next iteration of the process. The 4 Quadrant Test can help you take notes and record users' feedback. On a large sheet of paper, draw two intersecting lines to create four equal sections. Label each section with one of these four headings: *Likes, Dislikes, New Questions,* and *New Ideas.* As you observe the users and ask them questions, record the feedback in either the *Like* or *Dislike* quadrant. Then as questions come up, record them in the *New Questions* quadrant. And, when the testing phase sparks new ideas, record them in the *New Ideas* quadrant.

Reflecting on Results

This is the final step of the design-thinking process. This stage allows design thinkers to reflect on, or review and think about, whether or not their prototype solved the problem they defined. In the reflection stage, you should answer this question: Did the prototype meet the needs of the user?

Reflect on what you have learned, and talk it over with a group.

Reflection is part of the whole design process cycle—at every stage you must gather information, think about it, and make improvements. But the reflect stage is especially important because it requires you to think about how the idea and prototype could be changed or improved to better meet the users' needs. It is also the time to prepare for the next iteration of the process. Reflection may also show that the idea doesn't work and that you need to start over. Or it could show you small changes that could make a big difference.

Back to the Beginning

The first step of the reflect stage is to review all the feedback from users. Then ask two important questions:
1) What worked?
2) What didn't work?
Next, talk with your peers about the process. Review your work on the empathy and define stage and answer the following questions:
1) Did we meet the user's needs?
2) What needs are still unmet?

Recording your thoughts about the process and what worked and didn't work is a great way to reflect on the process.

Your answers to these questions will help you make plans for the next step. Because the design-thinking process is continuous, this information will help you start working on the next iteration. You will use this information when you start over with a new round of ideation!

What Have You Learned?

When you have found a solution that works for the user—whether that happens after one round of design thinking or several rounds—the reflect step is a good time to self-reflect on the design thinking process itself. Reflection can take many forms. You can write a journal entry, complete a

self-reflection checklist, or report your reflections using different media such as slides, a story, a video, or a drawing.

Reflection Questions

- What did you learn?
- How do you feel about your work?
- What patterns do you see?
- What surprised you?
- What could you do differently next time?
- What changes would you make to the process?
- What did others think of your solution?
- Did your solution work? What changes are required?

PROJECT:

Unequal Access to Information

We live in the **Information Age**. One of the main ways that we stay informed about our communities is by accessing information on the Internet. We also use the Internet to communicate with others, do our homework, and even apply for jobs!

Websites and social media platforms are popular ways to share and access information. To feel included in your own community, you have to know what's going on. Information about the people in your community, social events, special occasions, safety or emergency news, and government decisions are all important. For example, a city's website or social media page might post information about sports programs being offered at the community center or a holiday celebration scheduled in the local park. Or the city might have implemented new rules for the skateboard park that you want to know about.

However, only those people who have access to the Internet, know how to use websites, or have accounts on social media platforms can access the important information that is shared online.

There are many groups of people in communities that are still unable to access information online. This can be a barrier to their participation in their communities, because they may not be aware of events going on or social groups available to them. They may also be unaware of the services that are available to them, such as free language classes, apps that help differently abled people access the Internet, or programs that help low-income families purchase computers. Some of these groups can include:

- People who come to North America from other countries might not be able to speak English. It can be very difficult for them to learn English, which means they might have trouble interpreting written information online.

- Some people have **disabilities** that limit their ability to access online information. People who have visual impairments are often unable to read information online if a website does not include a read-aloud function. People who have hearing impairments cannot access audio information.

- People who have low incomes might not have the money or credit to buy computers, tablets, and smartphones. Many people also cannot afford to pay for an Internet connection or data services.

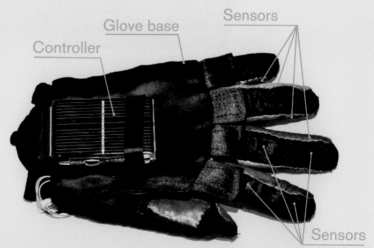

Meet some
CHANGE MAKERS

The Enable Talk Team

A group of young Ukrainian computer programmers have designed a pair of gloves that can translate sign languages into audio speech. These designers got the idea from observing some students at their school who have hearing impairments. These students were athletes and had a difficult time communicating with their hearing teammates who did not speak sign language. After building a working prototype that could translate a few signs into speech, the students won $25,000 at a competition called the Imagine Cup. They now plan to work closely with people who have hearing impairments to improve the glove's design.

Controller

Glove base

Sensors

Sensors

CASE

Language Barriers for Newcomers

Paw and Lah are **Karen refugees** from **Myanmar** (also known as Burma) who came to California with their children. They are eager to be successful in their new community, which is very different from the rural village they came from.

Paw and Lah speak Karen, Burmese, and Thai, but they only knew a few words and phrases in English when they arrived. Paw and Lah are working hard to learn how to speak and read English, but they are not learning as quickly as their children. They want to find

more free English classes. They also want to find good jobs, learn to use the local bus system, and maybe find a better apartment. And they have discovered that their children's school uses a website to communicate with parents. Everything they want to do seems to happen online, but they struggle to read information in their new language. They must ask their children to help them.

Paw and Lah rely on their children to help them read information online. But they know they need to learn themselves, too.

Language differences are a huge barrier to information access for refugees in many different communities.

- The United States has welcomed over 3 million refugees in the last three decades.

- Reading English is very difficult for Karen refugees from Myanmar because the languages they speak use a different kind of alphabet.

- Experts say it takes adults at least 360 hours of study to learn basic English.

The Design-thinking Process

Empathy What barriers do Paw and Lah face in accessing information in their community? How do these barriers affect them?

Define POV After you have used empathy to understand Paw and Lah's point of view, define their needs. Create a POV question that helps you begin to solve their problem.

POV QUESTION PROMPT: **How could we make it easier for … ?**

Who Gets the Message?

Amelia is blind. She goes to an **integrated school** and attends the same classes as students who are not blind. She has a large group of friends who use their phones all the time to talk and share stories. Amelia uses a **screen-reading program** to access the text on websites and her social media accounts. The technology reads every word on the screen out loud. This lets her send and receive text messages and tweets.

Amelia can post her own photos on Instagram and Snapchat, but she can't see the photos her friends post. She can only read

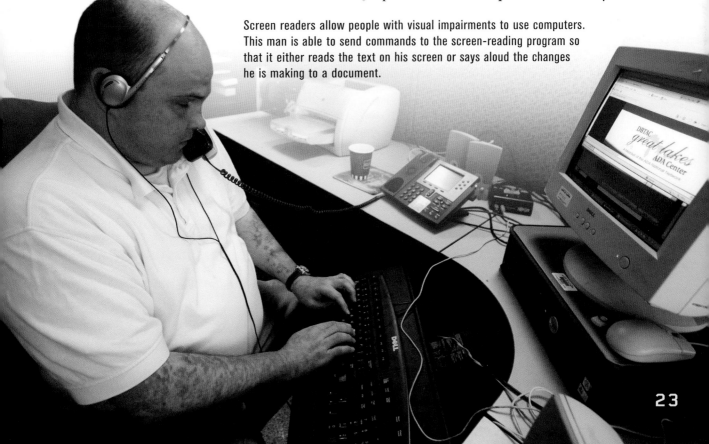

Screen readers allow people with visual impairments to use computers. This man is able to send commands to the screen-reading program so that it either reads the text on his screen or says aloud the changes he is making to a document.

captions and text from others, so she only gets part of the message. She often feels like she's missing out and doesn't really fit in with her friends.

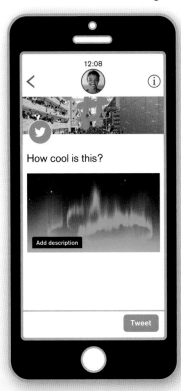 

Amelia's problems with using social media are similar to others.

- Over 8 million Americans have a visual impairment, which makes using a computer more difficult.

- Twitter has an "add description" feature for photos (above), but Instagram and Snapchat do not.

- Screen-reading programs cannot read text added to an image or in a typical **infographic**.

 ## The Design-thinking Process

Empathy What barriers stop Amelia from accessing information? How does this make her feel?

Define POV After you have used empathy to understand Amelia's point of view, define her needs. Create a POV question that helps you begin to solve her problem.

POV QUESTION PROMPT: **How could we improve … ?**

The Cost of Access

Dana cannot afford the cost of Internet in her home. She buys a pay-as-you-go data plan for her phone, but it usually runs out before the month is over. She finds it difficult to complete her day-to-day activities when her Internet runs out. Her daughter Cara's swimming lessons were filled by the time she got to the public library to do the online registration.

Dana cannot join online discussions with the other parents at Cara's school. Cara is often late with her homework because she can't get online. Dana worries Cara will fall behind in school. They also miss out on many of the free activities in their neighborhood because Dana cannot check her social media accounts very often, and this is where information about the activities is usually posted. Dana would like to find a higher-paying job, but most applications are done online. Dana is very frustrated by her lack of information and feels very disconnected from her community. The library is far from her home, and she doesn't usually have time to visit it to access the computers there. Sometimes, all of the computers at the library are full, and Dana does not have time to wait for them to become free.

Many people use computers available in public libraries to access the Internet.

Dana's situation is not unique.

- The cost for Internet access in the United States ranges from $50/month to over $120/month, which makes it unaffordable for many Americans.
- 33 percent of American households that do not have Internet access at home cite affordability as their main barrier.
- 90 percent of job applications have to be completed online.

The Design-thinking Process

Empathy How does Dana's lack of Internet cause barriers to her community involvement? How do these barriers make Dana feel?

Define POV After you have used empathy to understand Dana's point of view, define her needs. Create a POV question that helps you begin to solve her problem.

POV QUESTION PROMPT: **How can we help … ?**

Accessing Information

How can we improve access to information for everyone in our community?

It's time to put design thinking to work. Look back at the three cases of users who struggle to access information:

1. Paw and Lah from Myanmar cannot read English confidently and have trouble reading important information about their community online.
2. Amelia is blind and cannot see the photos her friends share on social media or read information about her community shared in photos and infographics.
3. Dana cannot afford Internet in her home, so she and her daughter have a difficult time participating in sports and activities in their community, and in succeeding at school and job searching.

Which user would you like to help? Choose either Paw and Lah, Amelia, or Dana's case and use the design-thinking steps to create a solution to their problem.

Empathize

Empathize to learn more about the user's point of view.
- Review the user's story, challenges, and frustrations.
- Learn more by watching videos and researching information in books or online.

Define

Use the POV prompt from the case study to define the user's need.

Ideate

It's time to brainstorm! Draw, sketch, or write down as many ideas as possible.
Organize your ideas and select one for the next stage.

Prototype

Create a prototype of your idea—keep it simple, cheap, and easy.
Remember that your prototype should be an experience.

Test

Show, don't tell—have your user or a peer test your prototype and give you feedback.

Reflect

Reflect on the results of your test.
- Has your prototype met the needs of the user?
- What can you change?

Reflect on the design-thinking process.
- What did you learn?
- What could you do differently?

Now, improve your prototype through another iteration of the process.
When you are happy with your solution, share it with your peers.

PROJECT:

Isolation in Communities

Many people have difficulty moving around their community, including older adults or people who have different physical or mental abilities. Other people may not have **social networks** because they live alone or do not have family or friends nearby. This commonly creates feelings of isolation and loneliness.

Isolation and loneliness are a problem everywhere. When people feel disconnected from their communities, they are less likely to participate in community activities and feel like they are important to others in the community. For some groups, isolation might be more common.

The United Kingdom has recently appointed a Minister of Loneliness to help combat loneliness in the country. Over 9 million people there report feeling lonely most or all of the time.

- As people get older, their lives change. Their children leave home, they retire from work, and they may experience changes in their physical and mental health. When these life changes happen, many people feel that they no longer have an important role, or purpose, in their communities.
- Many people have different physical abilities, which means that they require accessible buildings, parking lots, and restrooms. These are often required by law.

- But getting to accessible buildings is also a challenge when you have a physical disability. Sometimes it seems easier to just stay home.
- Adults who live alone might not have the support of friends or family when they need help. They also might feel lonely because they don't have another person to go out with and do things in the community, like go to a movie or eat in a restaurant.

Meet a
CHANGE
MAKER

Abigail Lupi and CareGirlz foundation

When Abigail Lupi sang and danced at her great-grandmother's 100th birthday party, she was able to talk to some of the residents in the nursing home and learned that living in a nursing home can be very lonely. But Abigail saw that her performance made the other residents happy. The positive feedback she got from her performance inspired her to create CareGirlz—a performance group of girls aged 6 to 13. CareGirlz sing and dance to help bring some happiness to others. They perform Broadway tunes and pop music favorites at children's hospitals, assisted living residences, and nursing homes throughout New Jersey.

CareGirlz is an organization that encourages girls to perform for people living in long-term care facilities.

CASE

Loneliness of Older Adults

Richard is 80 years old, and his life has a much slower pace than it used to. He retired from his job at the age of 65. At first, he enjoyed his retirement. Richard and his wife traveled to Europe and South America.

They also stayed active in their community by volunteering and helping to care for their grandchildren. But a few years ago, Richard's wife died. He tried to stay busy, but one of his sons had to move away for work, so he no longer has grandkids nearby. A little while later, he was in a car accident. After failing a medical test, his doctor had to take away his driver's license.

Richard now spends most of his time at home because he can't drive and there is no bus service near his home. His daughter comes to visit as much as she can, but she is very busy at work. Not only is Richard lonely, he also feels like he doesn't have a purpose in life. Richard used to start each day with a positive attitude, but now he often stays in bed most of the day, and he often tells his daughter that he doesn't feel well.

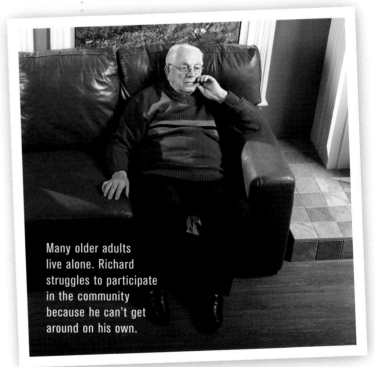

Many older adults live alone. Richard struggles to participate in the community because he can't get around on his own.

Richard is not alone.

- About 29 percent of the U.S. population over the age of 65 lives alone.
- 25 to 60 percent of older Americans, between the ages of 53 and 77, experience loneliness.
- Older people in poor health are twice as likely to report feeling lonely.

Empathy What things have lead to Richard's feelings of isolation in his community? How does Richard feel each day?

Define POV After you have used empathy to understand Richard's point of view, define his needs. Create a POV question that helps you begin to solve his problem.

POV QUESTION PROMPT: **How could we improve … ?**

CASE

Barriers for Differently Abled Persons

Lucy uses a wheelchair. She works in a building that is accessible, and her employer is very supportive. But Lucy cannot drive, and her local public transit system is not fully accessible. So, Lucy must use a special bus to get to work. This bus is part of the **paratransit** system in her city and takes her to and from work on a fixed, or unchanging, schedule.

If Lucy needs to go to the doctor, attend a birthday party, or go out for dinner with friends, she has to request a pick-up 3 to 5 days in advance. And the bus company can only provide a window of time for the pick-up. This means Lucy often arrives early or late, and then spends a long time waiting after an event is over.

Paratransit systems make public transit more accessible, but they can still be inconvenient and require a lot of planning to use.

max. 350 kg

Lucy has learned to plan her life around the paratransit system in her town for work and appointments. But because the system is such a challenge, Lucy often chooses to stay home instead of joining her friends. The most frustrating thing is that she cannot join her coworkers for unplanned lunches or after-work meet-ups. She would like to socialize with her coworkers more and worries that not joining in will effect her success at work.

Lucy is not alone.

- Over 2 million people in the United States use a wheelchair every day. Six and a half million people need a cane, a walker, or crutches to get around.

- 12 percent of people with disabilities have problems accessing reliable transportation, whereas only 3 percent of people without disabilities have the same problem.

- The Americans with Disabilities Act (ADA) requires public transit systems to provide services to people with disabilities.

The Design-thinking Process

Empathy How does Lucy's experience with transportation isolate her from her community? How does this isolation make Lucy feel?

Define POV After you have used empathy to understand Lucy's point of view, define her needs. Create a POV question that helps you begin to solve her problem.

POV QUESTION PROMPT: **How could we make it easier for … ?**

CASE

Isolation of Living Alone

Hannah is 38 years old and lives alone in a big city. She moved there after her divorce because she found a great new job. She is not very close with her own family, who live across the country.

She does keep in touch with friends from college on social media, but she doesn't have any close friends in her life. She has tried to make friends at work, but many of her coworkers live far away and commute to the office, or they are very busy with their families. It makes her feel sad to come home to an empty house with no one to talk to about her day. She used to love cooking with her friends and family, but now hates eating alone. She often stays home in the evening and on the weekends, because she feels uncomfortable going to community events alone.

Last month, she became very ill and did not know whom to call for support. She went to the store by herself to get medicine and soup, and she almost fainted. She had to take several days off of work, and no one except her boss called to see if she was okay. Now she wonders what she would do if she had a real emergency or needed help with something important.

Like Hannah, many adults live alone.

- One in seven American adults live alone, and that number is increasing.
- According to loneliness researcher John Cacioppo, 40 to 45 percent of people report feeling lonely.
- Census data showed that in 2016, 28.2 percent of Canadian adults lived alone—making a single-adult home the most common type for the first time since the census began.

The Design-thinking Process

Empathy What things contribute to Hannah's feelings of isolation in her new home? How does being isolated make Hannah feel?

Define POV After you have used empathy to understand Hannah's point of view, define her needs. Create a POV question that helps you begin to solve her problem.

POV QUESTION PROMPT: **How could we help ... ?**

Isolation

How can we prevent isolation and loneliness in our community?

It's time to put design thinking to work. Look back at the three users facing problems with isolation:

1. Richard is a 80-year-old widower who cannot drive his car and feels like he doesn't have a daily purpose.

2. Lucy uses a wheelchair and feels isolated because she cannot get around town easily to socialize with friends and coworkers.

3. Hannah lives alone, has a hard time making friends in a new city, and worries about not having someone to call on for help.

To combat isolation, special community events, like this one for people who are visually impaired, can be organized so that people have a chance to get out and socialize.

Which person would you like to help? Choose either Richard, Lucy, or Hannah's case and use the design-thinking steps to create a solution to their problem.

Empathize

Empathize to learn more about the user's point of view:
- Learn more by watching videos and reading articles.
- Ask questions about their needs.

Define

Use the POV prompt from the case study to define your user's need.

Ideate

It's time to brainstorm! Draw, sketch, or write down as many ideas as possible. Organize your ideas and select one for the next stage.

Prototype

Create a prototype of your idea—keep it simple, cheap, and easy. Remember that your prototype should be an experience.

Test

Show, don't tell—have someone experience your prototype. Observe your user's experience with the prototype and take notes on what works and what doesn't work.

Reflect

Reflect on the results of your test.
- Has your prototype met the needs of the user?
- What can you change?

Reflect on the design-thinking process.
- What did you learn?
- What could you do differently?

Now, improve your prototype through another iteration of the process. When you are happy with your solution, share it with your peers.

Challenges to Participation

Participating in the community is harder for some people than for others. To participate means to be involved in something, such as taking part in sports or groups or volunteering your time to help others. There are many barriers to participation that make it difficult for some people to really feel included in their communities.

It is difficult to join in when you don't understand something. Sometimes, the cost of participation is too high. Other times, cultural differences mean that some activities don't work for all community members.

If events or activities, such as fairs, sporting events, or volunteer activities, are not designed with everyone in mind, people can be excluded.

- Many people who are differently abled may be welcome to participate in events, but the event may not be accessible for them. So individuals who have different abilities may only get to watch rather than participate.

- There are many things that newcomers, such as refugees and immigrants, have to learn when they join a new community. Participating in special events, volunteer opportunities, and even everyday interactions in the community can be a real challenge when you don't yet understand the events or opportunities that are available, or how to participate in them.

Participating in local celebrations is one way that people can feel involved and welcome in their communities.

For some community members, participation in community events and programs is simply too expensive. People who have low incomes often cannot afford things such as ticket prices, program registration fees, sports equipment, or even transportation. Events and activities with high prices, or that require money spent on equipment or travel, exclude many members of communities.

Fouad Zaban Re-Designs Football Practices

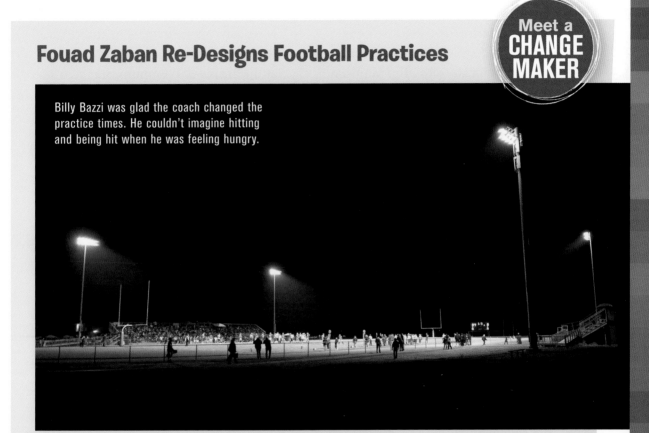

Billy Bazzi was glad the coach changed the practice times. He couldn't imagine hitting and being hit when he was feeling hungry.

Joining a football team is hard work. On some teams, members must participate in two practices a day during the pre-season. That's the case for the Fordson High School football team in Dearborn, Michigan. Many players on the team are **Muslim**. During the holy month of Ramadan, many Muslims fast from sunrise to sunset. This means that they do not eat food or drink water during the day. When Ramadan fell during the month of August, the players could not safely participate in pre-season training because they were fasting, and without food, had little energy to complete the challenging practices. So Coach Fouad Zaban and his coaching staff designed a new practice schedule to meet the needs of his team. The team practiced overnight—once at 11 p.m. and once at 4 a.m. Players could eat before and after practice and stay hydrated—then go home to sleep during the day.

CASE

Participation for All Abilities

Tony's son Madison has **autism spectrum disorder**. Because he is nonverbal, or does not speak, it is hard to communicate with him. Madison goes to school every day but cannot talk to his classmates or participate in traditional school activities. Madison is unable to participate in most community programs and events because they are not designed to support nonverbal participants.

Madison spends most of his time at home with his parents and younger sister.

Participating in everyday activities can be difficult for people who have different abilities, as they often need special help or **accommodations**.

It is difficult to find activities that Madison can participate in and enjoy. Building a relationship with Madison and learning to communicate in a variety of ways takes time. Most people don't understand how to become Madison's friend. Tony hopes to find a solution so Madison can participate with and connect to others in the community.

Madison is among many children who have autism spectrum disorder.

- In the United States, one in 68 children have autism spectrum disorder. Someone is newly diagnosed with autism every 11 minutes.

- Autism affects how people think, communicate, and behave. This makes it hard for people with autism spectrum disorder to interact with other people.

- According to the National Autistic Society, both children and adults with autism spectrum disorder often experience social isolation because they have difficulty socializing with others and may need extra support to participate in activities.

The Design-thinking Process

Empathy What things stop Madison from being able to participate in his community? How does this make his father, Tony, feel?

Define POV After you have used empathy to understand Madison and Tony's point of view, define their needs. Create a POV question that helps you begin to solve their problem.

POV QUESTION PROMPT: **How could we help … ?**

CASE

Language and Cultural Barriers

Ahmed has just arrived in the United States. He ran a shop in his small town in Syria, but he had to flee because of the **civil war**. He volunteered in the **refugee camp** where he lived. He organized activities for children and helped take care of older people in the camp.

Ahmed enjoys helping others and wants to do the same thing in his new home. Ahmed is taking English language classes during the evenings and would like to volunteer some of his time during the day.

Since he is new to the community, Ahmed doesn't know where to go to find out about possible volunteer positions. He has looked online for local volunteer organizations but his English skills make it difficult to understand the information on the sites. He knows he will need help filling out any required application forms, but he doesn't have anyone to ask for help. Ahmed wants to take an active role and contribute to his community and feels discouraged by the difficulties he is experiencing.

English language learning classes can help refugees and immigrants communicate using English. Knowing the language is a big part of being able to participate in the community.

Like many refugees and immigrants, Ahmed wants to learn about and give back to his new community.

- A survey of refugees in Minnesota shows that almost one-quarter of refugees don't know how to sign up for volunteering opportunities or feel they don't have the skills needed to volunteer.

- Volunteering is an excellent way to practice English-speaking skills in a real-world setting.

- Research shows that people who volunteer are more likely to be happy than those people who never volunteer. Also, people who volunteer a lot are even more likely to be happy.

The Design-thinking Process

Empathy What barriers does Ahmed face when trying to participate in his new community? How does being unable to participate make Ahmed feel?

Define POV After you have used empathy to understand Ahmed's point of view, define his needs. Create a POV question that helps you begin to solve his problem.

POV QUESTION PROMPT: **How could we make it easier ... ?**

CASE

Cost of Joining In

Julia is 12 years old and lives in Minnesota. Her parents both work very hard to pay for necessary things like rent, food, clothes, medicine, and transportation. They rarely have extra money at the end of the month. She likes to play ball hockey with her friends in the park after school, and she's been improving her skating skills.

All of Julia's friends at school play ice hockey. She desperately wants to join the local hockey league and play on a team, but her parents cannot afford it. Hockey is an expensive activity. Julia's parents cannot afford to buy her the necessary equipment, such as skates, sticks, helmets, and pads, or pay team registration fees and "ice time" fees, which cover the cost of renting a rink for practice and games. Julia's parents desperately wish they could help, but they know that the equipment and fees are just the beginning of the cost of hockey. They cannot take time off work to drive Julia to practice and games. Playing in out-of-town games and tournaments adds to the costs of travel and hotels. Julia wonders if she will ever be able to participate on the hockey team.

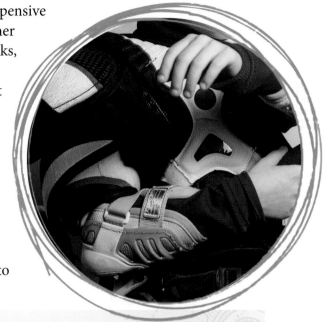

Julia and her family are not alone.

- In Canada, 68 percent of children in high-income families participate in organized sports. Just 44 percent of children in low-income families do the same.

- One in five parents in low-income American households report that their children's participation in school sports is decreasing because of registration fees.

- In a survey of more than 2,000 parents, 61 percent said that registration fees were a participation barrier, and 52 percent said that equipment costs were a barrier.

 The Design-thinking Process

Empathy How do Julia and her family experience barriers to participating in sports in her community? How does Julia feel when she is not able to participate?

Define POV After you have used empathy to understand Julia's point of view, define her needs. Create a POV question that helps you begin to solve her problem.

POV QUESTION PROMPT: **How could we make it possible for … ?**

Participation

How can we help everyone participate in our community?

It's time to put design thinking to work. Look back at the three users facing problems with isolation:

1. Tony is worried about his son, Madison, who has been unable to participate in community programs and events because they are not designed to support autistic participants. He hopes to find a solution so Madison can participate with others in the community.

2. Ahmed enjoyed volunteering in his refugee camp in Syria, because he enjoys helping people. But he doesn't know where or how to access volunteer opportunities in his new community.

3. Julia's family cannot afford for her to play hockey—a sport she loves and has been practicing with her friends, who all play. Julia wonders if she will ever be able to participate on the community hockey team.

Which user would you like to help? Choose Tony, Ahmed, or Julia's case, and use the design-thinking steps to create a solution to their problem.

Empathize

Empathize to learn more about the user's point of view.
- Review the user's stories, challenges, and frustrations
- Learn more about the user's problem by researching online, watching videos, and reading books.

Define

Use the POV prompt from the case study to define your user's need.

Ideate

It's time to brainstorm! Draw, sketch, or write down as many ideas as possible. Organize your ideas and select one for the next stage.

Prototype

Create a prototype of your idea—keep it simple, cheap, and easy. Remember that your prototype should be an experience.

Test

Show, don't tell—have someone test the prototype and ask them to give feedback.

Reflect

Reflect on the results of your test.
- Has your prototype met the needs of the user?
- What can you change?

Reflect on the design-thinking process.
- What did you learn?
- What could you do differently?

Now, improve your prototype through another iteration of the process. When you are happy with your solution, share it with your peers.

What's Next for Design Thinking?

We can use design thinking to meet big and small needs. Large organizations such as schools, businesses, and governments use design thinking. But you can also use design thinking to help make your local community better for everyone.

Get Involved in Design Thinking

Many organizations like the Henry Ford Learning Institute, the d.school at Stanford University, and IDEAco are bringing design thinking to schools. There are also workshops and camps you can join, and online tool kits for design-thinking projects. The City X Project is an international design-thinking workshop for kids, created by IDEAco. Design for Change is an international organization that has a design-thinking tool kit for kids and organizes an annual conference just for kids.

Next Steps: Designing for Accessibility

Thanks to the work of disability-rights activists, we have started to design solutions to make our communities more accessible. The law now requires buildings, services, and information be accessible to all. But instead of adding ramps and special technology, what if we designed everything with more users in mind? This kind of **universal design** will need lots of input from design thinkers who can empathize with many different kinds of users and apply the steps of define, ideate, prototype, test, and reflect. The future of inclusive communities is in their design!

Learning More

Alliance for Affordable Internet
An international coalition of institutions working to make Internet access more afforable for everyone.
a4ai.org

CareGirlz
Visit the CareGirlz website to watch videos of performances and learn more about the work they do.
caregirlz.org

City X Project
International design-thinking workshop for kids, created by IDEAco.
www.cityxproject.com

Connect2Affect
An organization committed to ending social isolation among seniors.
connect2affect.org

Design-thinking Guide
A guide for schools developed by Design for Change, an organization that believes children can drive change in their community.
designthinkingguide.weebly.com

Enable Talk Project
Learn more about the Enable Talk project and the groundbreaking gloves invented by students.
enabletalk.com

Henry Ford Learning Institute
Learn more about the design-thinking process from this institute devoted to education and community.
hfli.org

Refugee Center Online: Refugee Voices
Stories written by refugees and immigrants living in the United States.
therefugeecenter.org/refugee-voices/

StopGap Foundation
Learn more about what the StopGap Foundation is doing to ensure that buildings are accessible for all people.
stopgap.ca

The Ability Center
Learn more about the importance of inclusive communities.
www.abilitycenter.org/essays/the-need-for-inclusive-communities

The Tamarack Institute
An organization that helps to build vibrant communities through engagement and development.
www.tamarackcommunity.ca

Bibliography

Introductory Material
Design for Change. "Design-thinking guide." http://designthinkingguide.weebly.com/

Follett, Jonathan. "What is design thinking? Human-centered design and the challenges of complex problem-solving." O'Reilly Media, December 20, 2016. https://www.oreilly.com/ideas/what-is-design-thinking

Hicks, Bill. "Shanneil's Locker opens door for youth sports." *Daily Republic*, February 7, 2016. http://www.dailyrepublic.com/ solano-news/vacaville/question-shanneils-locker-opens-door-for-youth-sports/

Kreinbring, Lisa. "What is design thinking?" Henry Ford Learning Institute, June 19, 2015. https://hfli.org/what-is-design-thinking/

Kurtek, Sanela. "People of Toronto: Luke Anderson—StopGap Foundation." Torontoism.com, January 30, 2017. https://torontoism.com/toronto-people/2017/01/luke-anderson-stopgap

"The K12 lab wiki: Curriculum home page." Stanford d.school. https://dschool-old.stanford.edu/groups/k12/wiki/332ff/Curriculum_Home_Page.html

Wilkins, Dan. "The need for inclusive communities." The Ability Center. http://www.abilitycenter.org/essays/the-need-for-inclusive-communities/

"What is universal design?" Center for Excellence in Universal Design, 2012. http://universaldesign.ie/What-is-Universal-Design/

Project 1: Unequal Access to Information
Barron, Sandy et al. "Refugees from Burma: Their backgrounds and refugee experiences." Cultural Orientation Resource Center. Center for Applied Linguistics, June 2007. http://www.culturalorientation.net/content/download/1338/7825/version/2/file/refugeesfromburma.pdf

Bartholomay, Anna. "Language barriers challenge immigrants." USA Today, July 2, 2016. https://www.usatoday.com/story/opinion/2016/07/02/language-barriers-challenge-immigrants/86463812/

Brueck, Hilary. "Twitter wants everyone to 'see' your photos, including blind people." *Fortune*, March 30, 2016. http://fortune.com/2016/03/30/twitter-photos-for-blind/

de Castella, Tom. "How many hours does it take to be fluent in English?" *BBC News Magazine*, July 23, 2013. http://www.bbc.com/news/magazine-23407265

Dobby, Christine. "How Canada's Internet, wireless rates compare with international prices." *The Globe and Mail*, March 24, 2017. https://tgam.ca/2pdk8S4

Fernandez, Clarizza. "How to create an accessible infographic." Access IQ, September 27, 2012. http://www.accessiq.org/create/content/how-to-create-an-accessible-infographic

Graham, Sarah. "ConnectHome to expand to more than 100 communities."

EveryoneOn, May 30, 2017. http://everyoneon.org/2017/05/30/connecthome-to-expand-to-more-than-100- communities/

"How to make images accessible for people." Twitter Help Center. https://help.twitter.com/en/using-twitter/picture-descriptions#

King, Rebekah. "Making the case for connecting low-income residents to the Internet." NHC Open House Blog, June 13, 2017. http://www.nhcopenhouse.org/2017/06/making-case-for-connecting-low-income.html

Mabud, Rakeen. "Democrats promote Internet access, but affordability is the big issue." The Hill,. October 16, 2017. http://bit.ly/2EtdjW3

Olson, Parmy. "The amazing digital gloves that give voice to the voiceless." Forbes, July 16, 2012. http://bit.ly/2Gryq9G

Winn, Patrick. "The biggest group of current refugees in the US? Christians from Myanmar." PRI.org. May 4, 2017. https://www.pri.org/stories/2017-05-04/biggest-group-refugees-us-christians-myanmar

Project 2: Isolation in Communities

"Best practices for serving older adults living alone." Optimizing Aging Collaborative at UCSF. https://geriatrics.ucsf.edu/files/livingalonebestpractices.pdf

DePaulo, Bella. "What has changed for single Americans in the past decade?" The Washington Post, September 20, 2016. https://www.washingtonpost.com/?utm_term=.fd9961439f54

"Freedom to travel: Data analysis." Bureau of Transportation Statistics. https://www.rita.dot.gov/bts/sites/rita.dot.gov.bts/files/publications/freedom_to_travel/html/data_analysis.html

Hawkins, Kevin, PhD, Musich, Shirley, PhD, Wang, Sara, PhD & Charlotte Yeh, MD. "The Impact of Loneliness on Quality-of-Life and Patient Satisfaction Among Sicker, Older Adults." The American Journal of Geriatric Psychiatry, 23(3): March 2015. https://doi.org/10.1016/j.jagp.2014.12.176

Giannini, Robyn. "10-year-old shows how kids can give back." New Jersey Herald, February 24, 2011. http://www.njherald.com/article/20110224/ARTICLE/302249967

Leahy, Robert. "Living with loneliness." Psychology Today. February 9, 2017. https://www.psychologytoday.com/blog/anxiety-files/201702/living-loneliness

Meyer, Renee P., and Dean Schuyler. "Old age and loneliness." The Primary Care Companion for CNS Disorders, 13(2): 2011. https://www.ncbi.nlm.nih.gov/pmc/articles/PMC3184599

"Older Adult Drivers." Centers for Disease Control and Prevention. https://www.cdc.gov/motorvehiclesafety/older_adult_drivers/index.html

Prusak, Gabriel. A day in the life of lonely elderly woman and her trips to her senior center. The San Francisco Globe. Feburary 6, 2017. http://sfglobe.com/2015/10/27/a-day-in-the-life-of-lonely-elderly-woman-and-her-trips-to-her-senior-center/

"Rehabilitative and assistive technology: How many people use assistive devices?" Eunice Kennedy Shriver National Institute of Child Health and Human Development. https://www.nichd.nih.gov/health/topics/rehabtech/conditioninfo/Pages/people.aspx

Rieti, John. "Toronto Wheel-Trans riders singing the blues over delays, irregular service." CBC News. June 22, 2017. http://www.cbc.ca/news/canada/toronto/wheel-trans-concerns-1.4172574

Rosenbloom, Sandra. "Transportation patterns and problems of people with disabilities." The Future of Disability in America. M.J. Field and A.M. Jette, editors. Washington (DC): National Academies Press, 2007. https://www.ncbi.nlm.nih.gov/books/NBK11420/

"State of aging and health in America 2013." National Center for Chronic Disease Prevention and Health Promotion. https://www.cdc.gov/aging/pdf/State-Aging-Health-in-America-2013.pdf

Stromberg, Joseph. "Warning: Living alone may be hazardous to your health." Smithsonian Magazine, March 25,2013. https://www.smithsonianmag.com/science-nature/warning-living-alone-may-be-hazardous-to-your-health-8795790/

"U.S. Census Bureau facts for features: Unmarried and single Americans week September 20–26, 2015." U.S. Census Bureau, September 15, 2015. http://www.prnewswire.com/news-releases/us-census-bureau-facts-for-features-unmarried-and-single-americans-week-sept-20-26-2015-300143628.html

Young, Leslie. "Loneliness even unhealthier than obesity, should be a public health priority: psychologist." Global News, August 17, 2017. https://globalnews.ca/news/3678277/loneliness-even-unhealthier-than-obesity-should-be-a-public-health-priority-researcher/

Project 3: Challenges to Participation

"Autism prevalence." Autism Speaks. https://www.autismspeaks.org/what-autism/prevalence

"Autism quick facts." American Autism Association. https://www.myautism.org/all-about-autism/autism-quick-facts/

Cameron, Catherine. "Let's make sport affordable—so all kids can play." Tennis Canada. January 21, 2015. http://www.tenniscanada.com/lets-make-sport-affordable-so-all-can-play/

"Civic participation and social engagement among immigrants and refugees in the Twin Cities." Speaking for Ourselves: A Study with Immigrant and Refugee Communities in the Twin Cities. Wilder Research, July 2015. http://bit.ly/2tMIOGr

Clark, Warren. "Kids' sports." Statistics Canada, April 23, 2014. http://www.statcan.gc.ca/pub/11-008-x/2008001/article/10573-eng.htm#a2

"2017–2018 BYHA Fees (estimates)." Buffalo Youth Hockey Association. https://cdn3.sportngin.com/attachments/document/0102/8592/2017-18_BYHA_Fee_Schedule__FINAL___1_.pdf

Longman, Jeré. "All-nighters for a Football Team during Ramadan." The New York Times, August 10, 2011. http://www.nytimes.com/2011/08/11/sports/football/all-nighters-keep-football-team-competitive-during-ramadan.html?mcubz=3

Lowe, Alexandra. "Volunteering: A strategy for speaking more English." TESOL International Association, Feb. 3, 2016. http://blog.tesol.org/volunteering-a-strategy-for-speaking-more-english/

"Hockey equipment buying guide—For parents/kids." New to Hockey, September 28, 2016. http://newtohockey.com/hockey-equipment-buying-guide-for-kids/

"Pay-to-play sports keeping lower-income kids out of the game." C.S. Mott Children's Hospital National Poll on Children's Health, 15(3): May 14, 2012. https://mottpoll.org/reports-surveys/pay-play-sports-keeping-lower-income-kids-out-game

Saleh, Maryam. "English is Syrian refugees' 'key to survival.'" Medill Reports Chicago. September 29, 2016. http://news.medill.northwestern.edu/chicago/english-is-syrian-refugees-key-to-survival/

Segal, Jeanne, and Lawrence Robinson. Volunteering and its surprising benefits." Helpguide.org, October 2017. https://www.helpguide.org/articles/healthy-living/volunteering-and-its-surprising-benefits.htm

"Social isolation." National Autistic Society. http://www.autism.org.uk/about/communication/social-isolation.aspx

Glossary

accessible A place that is able to be reached or entered

accommodations Adjusting or adapting something to make it accessible to everyone

app A computer application, typically designed to be used on a mobile device.

autism spectrum disorder (ASD) A developmental disability that results in difficulties with social interactions and communication

brainstorm A group discussion used to create a list of ideas

civil war A war fought by people inside a country, usually between the government and a group of citizens

collaboration The act of working with someone to create something

community A group of people who live, work, and play together

disability A physical or mental limitation in a person's ability to move or sense the world around them

experiential Involving or based on experience or observation

failing forward In design thinking, learning from mistakes or failures to improve a process or other solution

grant An amount of money given by an organization or government to someone for a specific use

infographic An illustration that has lots of words and images to explain something

Information Age The period of history in which computers and digital information became very important

innovative Using new ideas or methods to improve something

integrated school A school where differently-abled children attend and learn in the same classes as children without disabilities

Karen An ethnic group from Myanmar and northern Thailand

Muslim Someone who follows or practices the religion of Islam

Myanmar (or Burma) A country in South East Asia, between Thailand and Bangladesh

paralyzed Being unable to move or feel part or all of a person's body

paratransit A public transit system that works alongside the main transit system to provide people with disabilities with access to public transit

refugee A person who is forced to leave their home because of war, natural disaster, famine or some other danger

refugee camp A camp where refugees live while waiting to return home or find a new place to live

respect Giving someone or something the attention and admiration it deserves

screen-reading program Software that reads all the text on a computer screen out loud

social network A group of people connected by social relationships such as friends, family, acquaintances, and coworkers

synthesize To bring together two or more parts to create something new

universal design A way of creating things such as buildings and websites that can be used by everyone

Index

About the Author

Rachel Stuckey is a freelance writer and
editor. She has worked as an editor in
educational publishing for over a decade
and has written more than 25 books for
young readers. Rachel travels the world
as a digital nomad and has recently
published an ebook about freelancing
on the road.